FINDING VALUE IN YOUR MESS

GETTING TO THE REAL YOU

BY:

CYLE E. CHAPMAN

CYLE E. CHAPMAN

Finding Value In Your Mess

ISBN: 061563902X
ISBN-13: 978-0615639024

Published by

C.E.C. Ministries, Inc.
Post Office Box 2418
Ventnor City, NJ 08406-2418
(609) 200-LIVE (5483)
www.cecministries.com

CYLE E. CHAPMAN

DEDICATED TO

Aurthetta M. Cone
Aka. "Granddear"

To my Mother
Sandramarie Boyet

To my Wife
Jennette Chapman

Special Thanks to
Jocelyn Boyd

I thank you all for your gifts of love...

CONTENTS

INTRODUCTION

I recently had the opportunity to speak at a Los Angeles County youth correctional facility for girls ages 13-18. All of the girls were on medication, and for some, this was not their first time at a correctional facility. As I began to talk with them I perceived that their major reason for being there was not because they did not know right from wrong, nor because they were misfits. I quickly realized that each of them did not understand the value of their life – the value of what God has placed inside of them.

Looking at the mess these young women were in, one may wonder how they got into this situation in the first place. Was it the lack of good parenting or the lack of good education? Could it have been a poor environment that caused these girls to turn to a life of crime? Although some, perhaps all of these circumstances may apply, the bottom line is that these young ladies did not know or even believe they had value. I asked, "How many of you have had someone close to you say that you were worthless?" Most of them raised their hand. But that was not what was most disturbing; the shocking fact was that many of them believed that they were worthless.

This led me to another question: how do we find value in our mess?

First, we must stop focusing on our mess – the negative things in our lives – and focus on this one simple truth: *"We All Have Value!"* The fact that we are living gives us value. *I recalled one of the lowest moments in my own life when I felt I had no value at all. No job, no money, and forced to move in with my mother after being on my own for over 10 years. I had no plans and no idea what to do with my life. All I could feel at that point was lost. I didn't talk to anyone because I was afraid to hear that I was a failure. But one night while sitting on my bed staring at a blank wall, I began to cry out. At that point I realized I had to do something with my life. So, I began to write down some goals that I wanted to achieve within one year. Then, I listed what I had to do to reach my goals, and then I got busy. Instead of staying depressed about moving in with my mother, I started focusing on how grateful I was to have a mother who allowed me to come back. Next, I had to focus on changing my situation by examining the mistakes I made and learning from those experiences.*

We must start forgiving ourselves for the mess we have caused. This is done by realizing that our past does not determine our future. Although this will be the hardest step to accomplish, it is achievable. We forgive ourselves by coming to the understanding of why we did what we did, and then making a decision to change that behavior. *Once I started down the path to change my situation, I had to forgive myself for getting into this mess in the first place. I made a bad decision that left me financially busted. Instead of doing what I knew was right and handling my business, I used my rent money to promote a party that I believed would make me famous. I listened to some friends (or what I thought were friends) talk about how they threw parties in a warehouse and made a killing. What I didn't know was that the parties they were throwing were illegal. On the night of the party I promoted, the police showed up and shut it down because we did not have a license. I* started hating my friends. I was the only one who had invested money in this deal. In addition, the police issued a citation and when it was all said and done, I was out almost $3000. That may not seem like much these days, but it sure was a lot of money back in the 90s. Nevertheless, that event changed my life.

We add more value when we do things that affect others in a positive way. *The more I looked back on that situation, the more it became clear to me that I couldn't be mad at anyone except myself. Yet, I still felt that my friends had gotten me into something where I lost money – not them. But, I was the one who put up the money and no one had put a gun to my head to do it. It was my fault for not doing any research because I thought I could make some quick money. Not only did I forgive myself, but I had to forgive my friends too.*

We must develop a desire for change and a desire for more in life . . . for more *value* in life. *For me, I had to look beyond my failures and realize that experience did not kill me. I had a roof over my head **and** the opportunity to change my situation. I found value in* *my mess by learning that even though something may look like a golden opportunity, it was my obligation to do some research first and continually do the right things. I desired to become the best at whatever I did in life by examining every angle.*

At this point, the healing process can begin. Healing, however, requires that we change some things in our lives, namely:

(1)   Our relationships with people

(2)   Our environment

(3)   Our attitude

(4)   Our focus.

CYLE E. CHAPMAN

1 CHANGING YOUR RELATIONSHIP WITH PEOPLE

One of the biggest stumbling blocks in realizing my value was in the negative relationships I kept. A negative relationship is one where there is no growth. Where you're always giving and never receiving. It is one where you are always being put down and never being lifted up. Negative relationships can also cause drug and alcohol abuse, illness, depression and even worse, suicide. They can also drive you away from healthy relationships and isolate you from the world.

There are people in this world whose solitary mission in life is to feed on the positive energy of others until there is nothing left but the waste (Negativity) they leave behind. These people mask themselves as someone who is interested in and supportive of what you are doing, but when they bite you and sink their teeth into you, they will leech until you are completely empty. At that point, you will not even realize your own value, and that is when the nightmare begins. When you wake up from this nightmare, you find out that everything you thought you had in this relationship is actually nothing at all. Your self-esteem will be in the toilet, your life in a complete mess, with no one there to pull you out. But it does not stop there. You will carry all those negative emotions into the next relationship and rob it of life – always on your guard waiting for any signs that will remind you of the last relationship, and then like a vicious dog you attack until you have killed all hope for a positive and health relationship.

I have been in relationships where I found myself always trying to please family and friends and never getting anything in return. One example of this was when I lived in Florida. I was in a relationship with this woman I will call Diana. Diana was about one year younger than me and still lived at home with her mother. I was co-owner of an entertainment company and at that time, I had it going on. Yes, I was paid. I had my own place, my own car and money to do what I wanted to do.

Diana and I dated for about two years and during those two years she was the best thing since sliced bread. At least that's what I thought. She knew just what to say, and just what to do, at just the right time. I fell in love with her from day one and never saw the warning signs. We got married and I gave her everything. Now when I say I provided a nice life for her, I mean I provided a nice life for her. She never worked, we had a nice place to live, she had all of the latest styles of clothes, fine jewelry, a car and she didn't even have a license, and access to the bank accounts. That was not a problem, because providing for my wife was what I was supposed to do. I had it, so she had it. But the problem was that every time I tried to grow it, she would spend it. Never saving or adding to it. She didn't want to improve her life at all. It got to a point that when the money got low (so she thought) she began to cheat on me. When I confronted her she would have the nerve to say, "It is your fault I cheated". She would then play the game card and have me believing it too. She was good and I wanted so much to make my marriage work. But all I was doing was working hard at making a lie work. I lied to myself and I believed that if I did it all, and gave it all, she would be happy and love me in return. But I now realize that was a lie and it almost cost me my life.

Negative relationships will drain every bit of positive energy you have and cause your value to decrease. It will cause you to accept life for what it is and not realize any changes that will cause you to grow. It will also have you do things you should never do, like mess up your credit, give keys to your home and let someone drive your car when they can't even afford to put gas in it. Now I am not saying that you should never do for a person. But if you find yourself always doing and never getting anything in return, then it is time to change some things in your life.

So, if you find yourself in a relationship and upon examination it has no benefits, you must LET IT

GO. I did and it was one of the hardest things to do at first. But I released myself from that bondage, that relationship which was choking the life out of me. My life started to change and my value increased. I began to reflect on the lies I told myself and realized how I never set boundaries in my relationship. People will only do what you let them do to you. You see, by me never setting boundaries, she was free to act anyway she thought she could and do everything she could get away with. It is easy for me to give you a list of boundaries I think should be in every relationship but every relationship is different. Likewise, every person in a relationship is different and will have their own level of what they will tolerate and what they will not.

Setting boundaries removes the guessing game from the relationship and allows each of you to grow, both together and individually. Now, once boundaries are set and someone crosses those boundaries, which everyone will at times, you have to stand firm and not allow your boundaries to be removed. If those boundaries continue to be crossed, then it is time to LET IT GO. You are greater than that and you should never give someone the power to change your value.

Changing your relationships take work, patience and standing firm. Just make sure you set boundaries that promote growth for both parties involved, not just YOU.

Taking Steps to Change the Values in Your Relationships

The first thing you have to do is evaluate where you are in life. You have to come to the realization that there is more in life than what you are experiencing right now.

Right now is the most important phase in your life and great effort must be taken on your part to be honest with yourself. Until you can be honest with yourself you will continue to develop relationships that end in destruction. Self-evaluation is to measure where you are to where you want to be. Create a list of where you are right now in your life. You should ask yourself the following questions:

How do I view myself right now?

_____

_____

_____

_____

Who are the three people I have the most contact with?

1._____

2._____

3._____

How do I positively affect their lives? (List the positive things you do which help them to grow)

_____

_____

_____

_____

_____

_____

_____

How do I negatively affect their lives? (List the negative things you do which stop them from growing)

_____

_____

_____

_____

_____

_____

_____

How do they positively affect my life? (List the positive things they do which help you to grow)

_____

_____

_____

_____

_____

_____

_____

2 CHANGING YOUR IMMEDIATE ENVIRONMENT

There are great deals of studies out there, which state that we are the products of our environment. They state that if you come from a poor family, then you too will be poor. Or if your parents are addicted to drugs and/or alcohol, then the likelihood of you being an alcoholic or drug addict is very high. Not to discount the countless hours and tax-payer money spent on these kinds of studies, but I disagree. The one thing they overlooked was a person's gift of choice.

Being poor is not the byproduct of our environment, it is the byproduct of our bad choices. We all have heard stories of people who went from rags to riches. If you were to interview any one of them, the one thing they would all have in common was that they made a choice to change their environment. Your environment does not direct your destiny; it is how you comprehend your destiny which creates your environment.

I am one of three boys raised by a single mother. Statics would show that we would be 1) more likely involved in gang activities, 2) one of us would have been dead before reaching the age of 21 and 3) have spent time in the prison system. Well, none of this was true for us. We have never been in the prison system, or involved in gang activities. All of us are alive and living the lives we created for ourselves. For me, it started with a choice. A choice I made not to believe what my environment said I would become, but to see myself open to new experiences that would help equip me to become the person I decided to become. I would not allow my environment to change how I viewed my life. I allow my view of life to change my environment. Yes, this is easier said than done, and to be completely honest, I made a whole lot of errors along the way. But what kept me going was my desire to realize my destiny. I accomplished this change by first, realizing the environment I was subjected to. Although my mother worked very hard sometimes working two jobs to provide the best for us, I was still exposed to certain elements around me that could've had a negative effect on my life. Like: gang violence, drugs and alcoholism and a world full of things a young man could get involved in. I looked at how allowing these elements into my lifestyle would affect my life in the long term.

Being apart of a gang, at that time, gave many of my friends the sense of belonging. You see, these gangs back when I was growing up did an awesome job recruiting young boys who came from broken homes. They thought brotherhood and the leader (known as the "Old G") became a father figure to young boys without fathers in their lives. The downside to being apart of a gang is the criminal activities in which they were involved. Drug dealing, fighting for turf, robbery and so on... All of these activities had results that never sat well with me. Like: going to jail, aiding in the destruction of families and lives through drug use (which has destroyed many lives), to dying for something that was not worth it at all. Looking at values (better yet, the lack of) I quickly realized that this lifestyle was not for me. This was one of just a few things I evaluated as I began to create steps to change my environment. To create change in your life you have to first look at what it is that you are exposed to, how this exposure can affect your life and your desire to not let that happen. I never wanted to see myself behind bars or dead before I had a chance to live. I had dreams of doing things, and accomplishing things no others in my family have achieved.

Another time in my life where I was forced to change my environment was when I was living in Colorado. I found myself, my wife and my daughter staying with my in-laws because a job I took did not work out. This was, to me, a very low point for a man that has had to make his own way for a large part of his life. Although her parents were great people and welcomed us with open arms, I knew that my welcome would not last long. So, I had to change my environment immediately. To start, I found a job that would require me to work at night when everyone was at home, and I would sleep for 4 hour during the day while they went to work and school. When I woke up, I went to the library to learn about how to build databases. You see, I was not able to go to school at that time so I taught myself. I then started to take my knowledge of computers to the next level. I learned how to use every piece of office equipment you would find in most corporate offices all at the library…Priceless. I knew that to be able to move my family to a nice place and provide a stable environment I had to change my marketability in the workforce. Within two months I had a good job and was able to lease a two-bedroom condo in a nice area. Changing my immediate environment caused me to learn something new and forced me to get active. From that experience, I learned that I can change other environments in my life that were decreasing my value.

Taking Steps to Change Your Environment:

As I stated earlier in this chapter, in order for you to change your environment you have to look at the elements within your environment and how they may affect your life. To do this, here are some questions you can ask yourself:

What are 5 elements in my immediate environment that is/can affect my life negatively?

1. _____

2. _____

3. _____

4. _____

5. _____

What makes these elements so attractive to me and why?

_____

_____

_____

_____

_____

What are 3 negative results these elements may produce?

1. _____

2. _____

3. _____

What are 5 steps you can do to change your immediate environment?

1. _____

2. _____

3. _____

4. _____

5. _____

What are the expected results to changing your immediate environment and when do you want to see them happening?

_____

_____

_____

_____

_____

_____

3 CHANGING THE PEOPLE IN YOUR ENVIRONMENT

Another area of your environment is the company you keep...your associations. This is different from changing your relationships. This change has to do with the type of people you are surrounded by. I'm sure you have heard the old saying... You are the company you keep. This was so true in my own life. When I started to look at the lifestyles of all the people I was hanging with, I could not find anyone that had a clear direction of where they were going in life. Most of them had the dreamer mentality. The dreamer mentality is when you envision yourself becoming something without actually working toward achieving that dream. Now there is nothing wrong about having dreams, but if your dreams never lead to reality then you are just replaying a fairy tale in your head. So I started to seek out those who were where I was trying to get to in life. To my surprise, it was easier than I expected. I started going to networking events and seminars where the discussions were focused on business, not on the latest video game or who was the finest actress on TV. At first it was very awkward for me, I felt like a small fish surrounded by sharks. I remember being at a networking event for business owners. There were about 50 CEOs in the room talking about best practices concerning starting up a company. Everyone talked about how they started their business and at that time I had no clue of what these professionals were saying. Every word went over my head. So I began to write down some of the terms they were using and the very next day I went back to the library to research those terms. I made up in my mind that at the very next event, which was scheduled every month, I would be able to have input in the discussion. I read book after book about starting up businesses. I learned about the ups and downs of being a business owner. I even started a business in the process. So when the next event came around, I was ready. I was the youngest person in the room and everyone started asking my opinion about various topics. I made a great deal of connections that day and my environment started to change.

So, if you find yourself surrounded by people that are not going where you envision yourself going, get with people who are. If you want to be rich and successful, stop hanging around people who are busted and position yourself around successful people. If you are tired of being single and jumping from one empty relationship to another, then connect yourself to married couples that have a clear understanding of commitment and love. Find out what they did to achieve the things you want to achieve. The power to change the people in your environment is the gift of choice. Choose to be a person of great value, walking in success, talking to successful people and watch the people in your environment change.

Steps to Changing People in Your Environment:

As mentioned in this chapter, you are the company you keep; to become a person of great value here are some questions to reflect on:

Are you the smartest, most successful and/or the person with the must value among those you hang around?_____

Who or what would you like to become and who and where do they hang out?

_____

_____

_____

_____

_____

_____

What networking groups are out there in the world that you can benefit from?

_____

_____

_____

_____

How can I benefit from connecting myself to these groups?

_____

_____

_____

_____

4 CHANGING YOUR ATTITUDE

Wow! This may be the most difficult change, because to change our attitude means to change what we do. And to change what we do we must first change what we believe. Our beliefs shape our attitudes toward things, people and even how we perceive ourselves. If we believe that the world is against us, then we will have an attitude of being against the world. If we believe that our lives will always be filled with hurt and devastations, then our attitude will be one that is destructive and hurtful. More than 50 percent of what we believe comes from what we continually deposit into our minds. When you do something long enough it will become your way of life. And when that happens, your attitude begins to take shape. But the good news is if our attitudes are linked to what we do and what we do is connected to what we believe, then we have the ability to change our attitude by first believing that we can have a positive outlook on life.

For many years I walked around with a negative view of relationships. I believed that if I could not have it my way then it was not worth having at all. I would place the standards for being with me so high that no one was able to achieve them. Yes, I was full of myself, and could not understand why people could not get it. I thought I was easy to get along with, would do anything for you, and was very giving on all levels. However, if you did not conform to my way of thinking, then you were kicked to the curb. I would just walk away from the relationship because I had a no nonsense attitude. I never learned that a relationship takes two people working to achieve a common goal. I was never taught that you have to put in the work to have a great relationship. When it came to changing my attitude towards relationships, I did not think I needed to. That is until I got tired of starting over again and again. As I got older, the dating scene was harder to deal with. I took a deep look into who I was and how others saw me. I started asking men that have been married for 20 plus years the question, "How did you do it"? And the overwhelming response was: "CHANGE YOUR ATTITUDE – IT'S NOT ABOUT YOU". That statement, as simple as it sounds, changed my life. It was a wakeup call that caused me to re-think how I viewed others as well as myself. It's not about you, means that although God created you to be special and entrusted you with gifts and talents, they were never meant for you to benefit from but for others to be blessed by them. To increase your value in life you must change your attitude from being about you to, "It's Not About You". Then you will start to focus on how you can bless others and others will start to bless you. Now I am not telling you to forget about how special you are or how talented you are, I am simply saying not to get full of yourself. In any relationship it takes two people to realize how special the other person is and how much that person impacts their life. Once you get to the unselfish, "not about you" stage of life, you will start to benefit from a productive relationship with people. You will start to create a positive atmosphere around you. You will start to accomplish more in life because you will no longer have an attitude of it's my way or the highway, but an attitude of how can I better myself so I can be a blessing to others and they can benefit from my gifts. Again, I believe that this is not the easiest change to make, but it is one of the most important changes in your life to make…Because it will change your prospective on dealing with people and life in general. In my own personal example of changing my attitude towards women, I first had to start by changing my attitude of giving myself, being unselfish in the relationship and then focusing on how to be a blessing to others. I am now in a very productive marriage where both of us are growing and benefiting from each other's gifts. I can honestly say that my life is fuller and I am unstoppable because I look to be a blessing so I can be blessed. My value is greater and my mess is less.

Steps to Changing Your Attitude:

How we perceive those around you and yourself are important, but just as important, is how others perceive you and your attitude towards things and/or them. Here are some questions to help you get started on changing your attitude:

How do I look at situations in my life that bring me discomfort?

_____

_____

_____

_____

_____

_____

_____

_____

_____

What am I repeating in my life and not seeing the desired results?

_____

_____

_____

_____

_____

_____

What are 3 things I need to change to affect positive results in my life?

1. _____

2. _____

3. _____

What are 5 benefits from having a changed attitude?

1. _____

2. _____

3. _____

4. _____

5. _____

5 CHANGING YOUR FOCUS

This changing takes a great deal of planning and effort, so don't rush it. You must first create a focal point. Your focal point is that one place or thing that all of your goals and objections point to. Whatever your focal point is, you need to set up a series of goals and objections to get you to that point of achievement you did not know was possible. One of the most important goals, and the first place you should focus on, is knowing who you are. Evaluate yourself by doing an assessment of your strong and weak points. You will need to be totally honest with yourself if you truly want to achieve your goal. Ask yourself some of these exploratory questions:

- What benefits can you bring to the table?

- What areas are you strong in?

- What areas are you weak in?

- What do you need to keep yourself engaged in this?

- What roles are you willing to play?

- What do you need to change about yourself?

These questions are just some of the many things you need to ask yourself before you start planning any area of your life.

Once you have examined who you are and have answered these questions, you can now focus on developing your value. If you are looking for a better job, look into increasing your skill levels first. The more you know the better job position you can get. When I was in high school I worked a summer job at a supermarket. I remember meeting a man that was a stocker on the night shift, let's call him Bob. While in the break room one night, Bob told me that he has been a stocker for over 20 years. Now my first thought was, wow 20 years, he must really like what he is doing. Then after further conversations, I found out that it was the only thing he was able to do. He would complain almost every night and when I asked why he stayed his reply was always the same, "Where will I go" and "What will I do". From hearing this statement I made up my mind that I would not be in that same position. Let me mention, it was not a lack of education on his part; he had a degree in business but nothing to go along with it. Having a degree is an awesome accomplishment and vital to achieve the life you may dream of, but if you do not have anything supporting that degree then it is just a pretty wall mount. I began to examine what I could bring to the table of any major corporation. What can I bring to the table? To answer this question I began to ask my managers and co-workers what were the two characteristics they liked and disliked about me. You have to write this down so that you can compare and come up with the two most common results. You can ask for more than two responses, but if you make your list too long you will get overwhelmed and talk yourself out of change altogether. So keep it short so that you get an accurate picture. If you look at your list and it is all over the place with no similarities, then that is an indication of a split personality and you need professional help.

For me, the two most common characteristics that they liked were my ability to learn quickly and willingness to do whatever it takes to get the job done. Now to my surprise, the two most common characteristics that they disliked was me not being more out-going in making a personal connection with my co-workers and managers and not managing my time well. I was shocked; I wanted to debate the issue, or just dismiss it but I did not. You cannot. This is another important part of changing who you are to increase your value in life. The perceptions of others will help you develop in anything you do. If you have ever been told that you should not care what other people think about you and you believed it, look at your life now and see if you are where you truly want to be. The perceptions of others should only be used to better you not destroy you. If someone has a negative view of you, which is based on fact, pay attention to it. Make every effort to change that view. Now if it is based on a preconceived notion and no facts to back it up, then toss it out and keep on stepping. Now if you hear this over and over again from different people, then you need to examine that view to see what you are doing or not doing to promote those feelings others have towards you. This is a great way to start your self-assessment. Remember, the more honest you are the better the change will be.

Once I completed collecting my data and compiled my list of likes and dislikes it became my strengths and weakness. Taking all of this information into account, I started with my weakness. As mentioned, one of the characteristics I needed to work on was my inability to make personal connections with others. Beginning to exam this vital flaw in my character, I found out that because of disappointment I had earlier in my life caused by others, I became a loner. I created a wall in my relationships that expected nothing from others to protect me from dealing with any form of disappointment I may have to experience again. I will go over disappointment in the next chapter, but this was what I found out to be the reason for not connecting with people. Now that I came to this truth about me, I started to look for opportunities to connect with them on a personal level. I made it a habit to celebrate their birthday with gifts and well wishes. If I was having an event like a party or just doing something fun and exciting, I would invite them to participate. Doing this, I began to make deeper connections with others, resulting in some awesome and fulfilling life long relationships. Now I looked for every opportunity to increase my skills and become more marketable. If there were a position I wanted at work, I would learn it first then volunteer to help out to show my stuff. Soon I found myself in that position ready to move to the next.

Steps to Take to Change Your Focus:

Changing your focus from choosing to look at life as it is, to what you want it to be will affect how your life will end up. Remember what you focus on you become. Here are some questions to help you examine what you are focused on and how to change it to get better results in your life:

What are 5 things in your life you continue to experience?

1. _____

2. _____

3. _____

4. _____

5. _____

Ask 3 people who are close to you what are 5 likeable and dislikeable characteristics?

*Person1:*_____

1. _____

2. _____

3. _____

4. _____

5. _____

*Person2:*_____

1. _____

2. _____

3. _____

4. _____

5. _____

*Person3:*_____

1. _____

2. _____

3. _____

4. _____

5. _____

What are the most common characteristics that these people like and dislike about you?

_____

_____

_____

_____

How can you focus on changing some of these
dislikeable characteristics to increase your personal
value?

_____

_____

_____

_____

_____

_____

_____

_____

_____

_____

6 CHANGING YOUR DISAPPOINTMENTS INTO STRENGTH

At some point in all of our lives we are faced with disappointment. Disappointment is an emotion that comes when something or someone has failed to meet our expectation or hopes for a certain outcome. Dealing with disappointment can leave us feeling discouraged, frustrated, worthless, embarrassed and downright angry. When these emotions consume us we tend to express ourselves in ways that are far worse than what disappointed us in the first place. So how we handle disappointment can make all the difference in how we recover from it.

Let's look at the life of one of my Purpose Living mentoring students. We will call her Denise. Let's see how Denise dealt with the disappointment caused by her husband's mistakes handling their finances. This is her story:

One day my husband and I sat down and created a plan on how we were going to handle our household finances. Our plan was that we would each be responsible for certain bills on a monthly bases. So for three months I was under the impression that everything was being taken care of. But to my disbelief this was not so. I was very upset that I could not stand to look at him. I began to lose my mind. I was filled with so much disappointment I exploded. I read him the riot act. I told him that he was worthless and failed as a man. I'm sure you could imagine some of the other words that were used that night. It was the worse argument we had. Nothing he could have said at that moment would have changed the situation, so I did not want to hear anything. So for about two hours I let him know just how I felt at the time, and just when I was gearing up for the third hour, he just got up and walked out the door and was gone for several hours. By the time he returned home I was sleep and did not even hear him come in. For days we did not talk and for months every time I got upset with him I brought up the situation again. I guess I was not over it...

Does Denise have a right to feel disappointed? Yes she does. Her expectations were not met creating a break down in trust. Does she have the right to get angry? Yes, anger is a natural response to disappointments and an emotion that we all feel from time to time. But how we deal with disappointments is what matters the most.

So let us look at six steps Denise could have taken to change her disappointment into strength.

Step One: Stop and calm down.

> When Denise found out that her husband's portion of the bills were not paid, her natural reaction was to get upset and to make sure he knew it. As humans we respond to negative situations with expressions of anger and aggression. This response was at some point in our childhood lives taught to us either directly or indirectly from our parents or someone close to us. We witnessed how our mothers reacted   to   difficult situations…How   our   fathers

exploded to news that challenged their position as the man of the family. We all have had some bad examples of how to react to certain disappointments. By calming down you are able to see clearly what really happened and begin the recovery effort. Remember death is the only time when all hope is gone. So if the situation did not kill you, you can gain strength and recover your hope again.

Step Two: Evaluate your feelings.

In further discussion with Denise we discover she did not even realize that her anger overcame her and how her reaction made the

51

situation worse. Once you recognize what type of emotional state you are in and how it can affect the situation, then you will be able to control that emotion so that it does not hurt you or someone else in the process of finding a solution. Your first thought should be, we all make mistakes and no one is perfect. By Denise's response to her disappointment she not only was unable to get to a resolution but now she has complicated the situation by creating a unsafe environment for her husband which caused him not to feel that he can come to her with problems.

Step Three: Talk it out.

Once Denise gains control of her emotional state she is now more adapt to work through the situation and get the results she wants. Having a discussion on what happen or did not happen in Denise's case would help regain perspective. Had Denise discussed what happened, she would have found out a situation occurred with her husband's bank account that caused a domino effect. He was a victim of fraud and although it was a correctable situation, the damage was done. Why did he not state this in the first place you ask? Well through further investigation, he did tell her and she blamed him for not paying more attention to his account. So you know with that weight heavy on his mind, he was not going to add to the insult. If you are not in a good emotional state with the person involved then talking to a neutral person can help also. This person may be able to help you see what truly happened and aid in the recovery plan. Remember not to focus on the emotions you are feeling, only deal with the facts.

Step Four: Reflect.

Ask yourself, is this something to really get upset and angry over? Is all hope gone in this situation? What was my part in this? What are the steps needed to recover from this. By truly reflecting on the situation one may find out that it was not as bad as it could have been. Denise would have found out that although the bills did not get paid then, her husband made arrangements with their creditors to catch them up next month. Nothing was lost, cut off or destroyed but the marriage. The energy spent reflecting on the situation is far less than the energy you will have to spend making up for losing your temper and healing the hurt you caused…If it can be totally healed.

Step Five: Learn from the experience.

It is through the mistakes we experience that make us stronger. Success is built on the mistakes we made and the way we respond to them.   When Denise discovered the mistakes her husband made she could have searched out the lesson in it. Since her husband does not review the account on a regular basis then she should help him by taking over that for him. Create a new plan which includes opening up an account just for the household bills. Most companies who offer direct deposit will allow you to split funds between two accounts. Now Denise is assured that the bills are getting paid. Denise's husband is made stronger because he is assured that his wife has his back.

Step Six: Stay positive.

Having the right attitude will determine your outcome. If Denise would have approached this disappointment with a positive attitude, her husband would not have left the house and feelings would have been spared. She would not have to seek forgiveness and the time wasted being upset with each other could have been spent getting closer. Have a positive attitude and you will see that failures are meant to make us better. And when we are better, disappointments fade away. Remember, how you react to your situation will directly determine the outcome. In other words, if you react positively your outcome with be positive. But if you react negatively then...

Again, death is the only time when all hope is gone. If you are still living there is still hope. If there is still hope, you have what it takes to change disappointment into strength.

7 LIVING WITH YOUR CHANGE

One of biggest challenges in my life was living a changed life. Taking all that I learned and applying it to my life was more than a notion it was real work. Losing possessions I thought I could not live without. Cutting ties with people I thought played an important role in my life. Leaving behind habits at the time I believed was the norm. All of this was frustrating at times and left me wondering if it was all worth it. But the rewards outweigh the emptiness and hard work it took to create a life that increases my value instead of decreasing it. Plus, I realized that the very things I was trying to hold on to were the very things that were killing me inside and out.

So how do you live with your change? This is a question in which many people ask me. To answer this, here are some pointers that help me live a life of greater value. I began to believe in myself, that everything is possible and failure is not an option. The only true failure is when you give up. As long as you keep trying you will eventually achieve what was once impossible for you to achieve. Remember that great childhood story someone told you about the little engine that could? Because of his size and situation that little engine did not believe that he could pull a heavy load like the bigger trains. But one day the little engine made up in its mind that it can be done. He saw himself doing the impossible so much so that he began to pull a load bigger than himself. I think I can, I think I can the engine cried out as he pulled the heavy load up the hill. I think I can, I think I can, I think I can…. as he began to climb higher and higher up the hill.

This is the same attitude that you must have when you are faced with the hills of life. I think I can change the relationship I keep with people. I think I can change the environment I'm in and even the people in it with me. I think I can have a better attitude toward life and my situation so I can learn some valuable lessons and live a productive life. I think I can change what I focus on and handle my disappointments in a way that produces a purpose filled life.

No matter what situation you are currently in you can change it. You just have to want it bad enough to put in the work. It is not something that will happen for you overnight. Changing my life to what it is now was a process. A process worth taken because all of the wonderful experiences I gained along the way.

"In Christ Jesus, we can do all things".

This is the message I speak to myself every day. You can change how you look, where you live and even the people you hang with. But to change who you are, you must first change whom you believe in. I used to believe in me and me alone. I believed that everything I had and did was because I did it. And I was half right. The mess I created for myself was directly because of the idea I had in my head that I can do anything I put my mind to; but the problem with that was I forgot that I had a purpose in life, and doing anything that went against it was like flying a plane with no wings. Yes, I could taxi down the runway but without wings I never left the ground. I had many great ideas and tried many things but all never left the ground. But when I began

63

to realize my purpose in life and things I needed to do to live in my purpose, I found my wings and began to fly.

All of us are born with great value in life. From the time you came out of the womb your life took shape. What happened was from the time you began to learn what life was all about, you created images in your mind of what the good life is. We were taught that we should be doctors, lawyers, police officers and firefighters, without ever researching what we were created for. Finding value in your mess is all about changing how you look at yourself and your situation. You are valuable no matter what happened to you and no matter what you have done. Living a changed life is worth everything you have gone through to get there. Stop focusing on the: "What happen and why it happen". Start focusing on how I can change what happened to see you living a life filled with purpose and

value.

ABOUT THE AUTHOR

Cyle E. Chapman has inspires thousands of people a month to live the life they were purpose to live and to make necessary changes in their life to experience maximum potential. He's shared the stage with Jewel Diamond and some of the most respected teachers, community and religious leaders of our age. His clients have included executives and entrepreneurs around the country.

Cyle is the rare trainer capable of coupling personal change with purpose living development which is why thousands of people seek him out for Life Coaching.

Licensed and Ordained, Cyle Chapman is the Founder and Senior Pastor of New Grace Worship Center and C.E.C. Ministries, Inc. in Pleasantville, NJ. He is also a Board Certified Faith-Based Clinical Therapist as well as a Certified Behavioral Assistant

What is Life Coaching?

Life Coaching is a profession that is profoundly different from consulting, mentoring, advice, therapy, or counseling. The coaching process addresses specific personal projects, business successes, general conditions and transitions in the client's personal life, relationships or profession by examining what is going on right now, discovering what your obstacles or challenges might be, and choosing a course of action to make your life be what you want it to be.

How does it work?

Life Coaching is a designed alliance between coach and client where the coaching relationship continually gives all the power back to you, the client. We believe that you know the answers to every question or challenge you may have in your life, even if those answers appear to be obscured, concealed or hidden inside.

* Complimentary Coaching Consultation
* 60 minute phone call per week
* Unlimited Email support
* Occasional brief check-in calls

Seminar/Worships

Cyle's signature topics and presentations include:

* Getting to the REAL You: Finding Value In Your Mess

* Living Your Divine Purpose: Recognizing and Developing Your Purpose

* The Power of Leadership: Unleashing the Leader in You

For more information or to contact the author go to www.cecministries.com

www.ingramcontent.com/pod-product-compliance
Lightning Source LLC
Chambersburg PA
CBHW071421040426
42445CB00012BA/1235